Katy —

Love and God's blessings to a sweet friend

Ruth Cox

Words In The Key Of Me

by

Ruth Ann Trent

Bloomington, IN  Milton Keynes, UK
authorHOUSE

AuthorHouse™
1663 Liberty Drive, Suite 200
Bloomington, IN 47403
www.authorhouse.com
Phone: 1-800-839-8640

AuthorHouse™ UK Ltd.
500 Avebury Boulevard
Central Milton Keynes, MK9 2BE
www.authorhouse.co.uk
Phone: 08001974150

© 2006 Ruth Ann Trent. All rights reserved.

No part of this book may be reproduced, stored in a retrieval system, or transmitted by any means without the written permission of the author.

First published by AuthorHouse 7/10/2006
ISBN: 1-4259-3896-5 (sc)

Printed in the United States of America
Bloomington, Indiana

This book is printed on acid-free paper.

Also published:

Get It, A Pocket Pilot Career Navigation Guide 1st Books, Bloomington, Indiana, 2002

A Book of Poems - Ruth A. Trent
Hand copied and illustrated by
Barbara Smith December 1979

Dedicated to:

My long-time friend and lifetime sister...
Lillian Jean Fishman Villella Vegotsky.

There is no description for our relationship;
we are more than friends. No two people
ever laughed, cried, screamed, and cursed
the world together as the two of us have. We
love our sons, and give them our best. We
have crossed some of the same life lessons,
taken two different paths, and ended up
with the same results...what a hoot!

We can go for long periods of time without
seeing or talking to each other, and
pick up exactly where we left off in our
last encounter. We think differently, yet
we think alike. We have always totally
embraced each others' spirits. We lift each
other up when we are down... 3,000 miles is
no deterrent to this relationship.

We have shared the lessons from our
different experiences in order to support and
console each other. We've shared with each
other wisdom and laughter. Lillian was
the inspiration for many of my ditties. God
bless you my sister. I love you –

Ruth Ann

In Memory Of...

Delores Costello Trent-Sims "Lois", my sister, who has transitioned from this world to the next realm after a valiant battle with Cancer. I will miss her as a friend and as a sibling.

Lois was unique with her own distinctive style and view of life. She was a willing soul, and a loving sister to me. I don't know if she ever recognized what were her real gifts. I never knew anyone who could take life "in stride" as she did. When she became enthralled with something, she gave it her all. She made contributions to the lives of many who crossed her path. I know that she will greatly enhance the dimension in which her soul resides.

"Enjoy the next journey, Lois. I will miss your earthly presence, but will carry your spirit within my heart until we meet again".

Love, Ruthie

TABLE OF CONTENTS

PROLOGUE xv

NAVIGATION I — Get It Down To Basics...as Simple As A-B-C 1
ABCS OF GETTING IT- CHOOSING YOUR CAREER 2
ABCS OF GETTING IT - NAVIGATING YOUR HEALTHY WEIGHT 13
ABCS OF GETTING IT – RELATIONSHIPS 23
ABCS F GETTING IT – RAISING CHILDREN 29

NAVIGATION II – It's Personal 37
WHY AM I HERE? 38
THE DECADE OF MY EVOLUTION 43
ON THE WINGS OF PRAYER 45
MY MARRIAGE 47
OUT OF NOWHERE, AN "ANGEL" 49
WITHOUT FATHER 52
FIFTY-EIGHT, PLUS ONE 54
THE RELATIONSHIP GENE 56
FIGMANTS 59
ODE TO MOTHER 60
THOUGHTS TO MYSELF 62
LIFE'S JOURNEY 63

MORE THOUGHTS TO MYSELF 64
GIVE ME STRENGTH LORD 67
A TRUE GIFT OF LOVE 70
MINDSET 71
HOW DO YOU FEEL, LORD? 72
WHY 74
FEELINGS 75

NAVIGATION III – The Children 85
A CHILD 86
I HAVE FEARS 88
DEAR CHILDREN 90
HEARTBREAK 93
A LETTER TO DAVID 95
COCAINE 97
EVELYN LORENA AND HER CREDIT 99

NAVIGATION IV – Oh, It MUST be Love! 103
MY CHANGE HAS COME 104
SPRING IN DECEMBER 105
LOVING HIM IS… 106
LOVE SICK 107
WHEN YOU FIND THAT MAN 108
WE CAN 110
MY VALENTINE 111
MY BAHAMA BABY 112

IT'S POSSIBLE 113

NAVIGATION V – The Love Is Gone! 115
WHEN IT IS OVER 116
DYING LOVE 118
JUST SO YOU KNOW 119
TIRED 120
APOLOGIES.. 121
PLAYING THE WHEEL OF LOVE............ 122
TRUST.. 123

NAVIGATION VI – Pot Pourri 125
STRESS... 126
CLOUDY DAY CHRISTIANS.................... 129
DON'T GIVE UP..................................... 130
RIDE, RIDE, RIDE 131
KEEP TO THE PATH 133
FOR CREW COLUMBIA 134
FORGIVENESS 135
CHOICE.. 136
SPRING FEVER 138
EPILOGUE.. 141
REFERENCES 142

PROLOGUE

Songs are but poetry married with tones and rhythms. Poetry teaches, bemoans, exalts, heralds, chides, defames, embraces, and motivates. It can be a great release, a panacea for depression, or wings on which to fly expressions of life and self.

My poetry writing began as homework in Mr. Loper's 5th grade class. It was a writing assignment that I chose to express in verse. I entitled it 'My Love For You' ...I was immediately hooked.

> I love you in the morning
> I love you late at night
> I love you at mid-day
> Under sun shining bright
>
> I love you when you're happy
> I love you when you're sad
> I love you when you're serious
> And even when you're mad
>
> I love you not for money
> Nor for the things you do
> I love you simply, purely,
> And just because you're you

My next opportunity came in the form of support to a very dear friend. Whenever life dealt her a blow that saddened her, I would express my support or disdain for the situation through a poem on her behalf. That was over 40 years ago, and as my friend and I reminisce about times past, we can benchmark various eras and relationships in our lives by some of those poems.

Eventually, I began writing poems as a personal release. Since I am an extremely internal person, oft times I did not want to share my feelings even with those closest to me. Writing was always so great a vent. Very often my output was related to my love life, or lack thereof. Other times it was just frustration with life, the world around me, and the puzzlement of trying to find my place in it.

Sometimes I would write from sheer joy. Too often I would think poetically as I observed nature, children, or love in any form, but I did not stop to write it down. That I regret. I should have always had paper and writing utensils at the ready. When we take the time to notice, life is SO worth expressing poetically. Listening to the "masters" of music motivates me to write about what I hear, but I can be too overcome by the beauty of compositions, or find myself at a loss for any words to describe the sounds of Mozart, Bach, Handel, and even more contemporary composers and artists. Music is its own form of poetry so I need not be redundant. But sometimes I am moved to consider it.

**NAVIGATION I — Get It Down To Basics...
as Simple As A-B-C**

ABCS OF GETTING IT- CHOOSING YOUR CAREER

From GET It! A Pocket Pilot Career Navigation Guide by Ruth Ann Trent, 2002

Avoid negative people, places and habits
Believe in yourself
Create your own priorities
Dare to dream
Encourage yourself when no one else will
Faith and fear cannot room together
Grant yourself a margin to err
Help others (what you give comes back to you)
Ignite the flame of hope daily
Judge no one
Karma…take it seriously
Love yourself first, then infect others with love
Marry your dreams to your goals
Navigate through life with a sense of purpose
Obligate yourself **to** yourself
Practice and prioritize that which is healthy for you
Quitting is not an option; make a wise decision to stop
Reject that which is not good TO you, or FOR you
Stand on the promise of the Universe
Take control of your destiny

Words In The Key Of Me

Understand yourself and then try to understand others
Visualize the journey to envision your destination
Waste no time lamenting what you cannot change
X-ray your feelings, and see them through honest eyes
Yield, when you must, with strength and dignity
Zig and **Z**ag as you and need to…flexibility is an asset

∞ ∞

Avoid negative people, places and habits —

Take this statement exactly for what it says. Do not surround yourself with negative people or negative energy. Quite simply, it does not add joy, progress, or happiness to you to be brought down by others. If someone is having an off day or an off moment, you can withstand their negative mood and maybe even try to help bring them out of their doldrums. But if someone who is constantly in your "space" carries with them a negative aura, you need to get away from them. They will block your life's light from shining through. They will bring you down, and eventually infect you with their negative attitude. Nothing positive comes from constantly looking on the dark side of things, and always feeling downtrodden. Positive energy and environments breed positive outcomes.

Believe in yourself —

If you must, go to your mirror each morning and say an affirmation to your image. If you need to sit and meditate to a self-positive mantra, then do it. Bring into your deepest knowledge what a wonderful creation you are. As human beings we are quite a magnificent entity. Know that and believe it. When you truly discover the power of

Self, allow confidence and belief in your capabilities to reign. Let no one tell you what you can or cannot do; let no one place limitations on your aspirations.

Create your own priorities —

Empower yourself to control your life-schedule. You might have persons to whom you report in various aspects of your existence, but do not give them control over you. Only you should prioritize your life. When you set your priorities, do so with all knowledge of whom you are and what you need. Do so with respect and consideration for those whom your life-schedule will impact, but do so with the assurance that you are the correct person to make such decisions.

Dare to dream —

If you have **no** dreams, you might as well just give up now! Whatever you want that has not yet been attained, dare to dream it. Dreams are blueprints, and if you dare…you can build them into a reality.

Encourage yourself when no one else will —

Remember the 'Little Engine That Could'. Be self-reliant. Know your strengths. Trust your own instincts. It *is* acceptable to pat yourself on the back. Be your best fan. Cheer yourself on!

Faith and fear cannot room together —

Faith needs to cancel out fear. Have faith that you need not be afraid. The only way to perfect your faith is to test it. The more you test it, the stronger it becomes. **F**amily and friends are for support – Invite family and friends to rise to the occasion of being a strong support system. Do the same for them. Don't be false with them, don't lie to them, don't live in denial around them, and don't be untrustworthy. If you value family and friends, they will support you when you need a soft place to fall, a sympathetic ear to listen, or a strong arm on which to lean.

Grant yourself a margin to err —

Unless you created the universe, unless you can walk on and calm raging waters, unless you arrived via an immaculate conception, then don't expect to be perfect! Plain and simple, you are human. You will make mistakes. What you do **after** making the mistake is more important than the error itself.

Help others (what you give comes back to you) —

When the universe offers you the gift of assisting someone, <u>accept the gift</u>. By helping someone else, you will reap untold rewards. You will see an unforgettable look in someone's eyes; you will see smiles of the brightest magnitude; and you will experience the warmth of appreciation in someone's heart. But, the greatest gift of all will be when it is offered back to someone you love.

Ignite the flame of hope daily —

As each new day dawns, have hope that it will be the best day so far. If you ignite such hope, you will exhibit attitudes and activities that will allow it to come to fruition. As you hope for world peace, be an individual peacemaker. As you hope for more love, function in a loving manner; as you hope for success, clothe yourself in a successful demeanor.

Judge no one —

Personal Judgment is only your opinion. The opinions you possess, unless asked, are usually best kept to yourself. Verbal judgment is virtually gossip, and gossip is harmful and can be mean-spirited. Judgments and gossip hurt not only the recipient, but also the donor. Rise above it... spend your thoughts and energy in other positive ways.

Karma...Take it seriously —

It is life's boomerang. If you don't believe that, you had better duck as you walk, and keep an eye over your shoulder!

Love yourself first, and then infect others with love —
You cannot give what you do not embody. Love yourself first, so that you can appreciate love for and from others. You will then be strong enough to give love without reservation. And, *true* love is not given any other way.

Marry your dreams to your goals -
Just as you should choose your career with your heart whenever possible, so should you incorporate your dreams into your life as goals. If the dream is worth dreaming, set a plan in motion to make it come true.

Navigate through life with a sense of purpose -
Unlike winged creatures, we cannot fleetingly fly through life and aimlessly land at a destination. Sooner or later we must take root, lay plans, define order, and make connections. Even if our plan involves moving from place to place, we need to know how to get there and why we are going.

Obligate yourself ***to*** yourself -
Commit to living your life in *your* best interest. You must commit to your physical, mental, and spiritual health, at the highest possible level. If you can do that, all other obligations will be simplified.

Practice and prioritize that which is healthy for you -
Again, self-preservation and self-priority impact every other phase of your life. The more you wrap arms around self, the bigger the muscles you will have to wrap arms around others and life situations.

Quitting is not an option; but a wise choice to stop **is** -
Giving up and abandonment are inherent in defining the word quit. The consequence is not in the act of discontinuing, but in doing so thoughtlessly.

Reject that which is not good TO you, or FOR you -
Surrounding your self with things, people, or activities, that are not useful, positive, or meaningful, is a waste of life. Use your **P's** *practice/prioritize* **and Q's** *quitting is not an option, but a <u>wise</u> decision to stop can be a good option.*

Stand on the promise of the Universe -
We are man. We are the product of God. We can walk, talk, think, and create. What more can we ask?

Take control of your destiny -
Start a personal corporation, having *me, myself,* and *I* as the executives. Devise your mission statement with the CEOs in mind. Conceive a plan from talents and dreams. Schedule the necessary preparatory training, and consult with appropriate advisors. Then, work your hardest to achieve happiness and success.

Understand yourself then try to understand others -
Much like love, you must own it to give it. If you don't understand how you function, you will have little success interfacing with others. Your prospective will be skewed and your vision narrow. When we perform internal scrutiny, we are often awakened to the meaning of the behavior of others.

Visualize the journey, to recognize your destination(s)-
Know what you are seeking. Envision the outcomes. Inquire of those who have been there before you. Study what you can about where you want to go. When you arrive, the

landscape might not be exact, but you need to be able to recognize it.

Waste no time lamenting what you cannot change -
Acceptance of the reality is like having a savings account. You may not save money, but you save heartache, misery, time, and pain. If we learn lessons of things we cannot change early on, it saves us time to spend on other priorities.

X-ray your feelings, hold them up to the light, and look at them through honest eyes - Be honest with yourself. Self-denial serves no purpose. If we are most honest *with* ourselves, *about* ourselves, others can hurt us less. Express feelings in truth, after first examining them honestly.

Yield, when you must, with strength and dignity -
Sometimes we have to give in. When that occurs,
it is important to do so with stamina and pride. Sometimes one yields to be the bigger person, or for the good of another. Know when to hold 'em and when to fold 'em.

Zig when you need to zig, and **Z**ag when you need to zag...flexibility is an asset —

Ruth Ann Trent

Life is not a straight path without obstructions. We often have to lean to the left or lean to the right. If we attempt to go through it without deviating, we will be broken into pieces from walking into walls.

ABCS OF GETTING IT - NAVIGATING YOUR HEALTHY WEIGHT

Assert Your Inner Strength
Breathe
Challenge Yourself
Discard Non-supportive People
Evolve
Feel what you feel
Goal Set
Honor Your Spirit
Invest in You
Join people or activities supportive of your goals
Kindle New Friendships
Learn from Mistakes
Motivate yourself; Mirror the aspired behavior
Navigate through issues of impact
Operate From Your Power Base
Patience…practice it
Quitting cancels your reward
Resilience…make it your middle name
Stay Focused
Think Through the Process
Understanding, Understanding, Understanding
Value the Journey
Wean & work
"X" is not to be anywhere in your clothing size

Ruth Ann Trent

Yern for the way you want to be
Zest – Add some!

ABCS OF GETTING IT- NAVIGATING YOUR HEALTHY WEIGHT)

Assert Your Inner Strength – Modifying your behavior is not necessarily going to be easy. It is *not* unnatural to decide to make a change, and then subconsciously resist that decision. Our very own bodies might be the first line of opposition. Some body parts will scream for salt, sugar, or carbs. Others might bemoan the muscle aches. Even with a made up mind, expect internal resistance. You must, however, master your domain and assertively hold ground to your commitment.

Breathe! – First breathe a sigh of relief that you have come to your senses and revered your person enough to consider your own well being. Next, breathe... literally! Deliberately breathing and re-circulating Oxygen is an excellent practice. Pilates, Yoga, and many other fitness disciplines emphasize the importance of breathing rituals. When one is stressed, deep and/or steady breaths are a remedy. Research the benefits of breathing and incorporate it into your plan along with your normal "functional" breathing. Oxygen flow is important; breathing drives the flow.

Challenge your self – The initial challenge is that of change. Change your way of thinking, your old habits, your movements, and possibly your physical and human environments. Challenge yourself to commit to discipline, emotional stretching, emotional healing, love and respect of your own will, and acceptance of your personal power. Challenge yourself to a higher measure of success.

Discard Non-Supporters - Separate the "wheat from the chaff." You are undertaking this metamorphosis for yourself. Therefore you need no other agreement. Kick "naysayers" and saboteurs to the curb.

Evolve - Do not expect to pursue and conquer instantaneously. You must evolve through this change process. Embrace the ups and downs. Inhale the exciting ride along the way to fulfilling your goals (as the journey unfolds, it will become more and more enjoyable). Stop and seize the personal growth. Document the process via journaling and photography. Evolution is historical and memories can be educational *and* motivational.

Feel – Feel good, feel depressed, feel scared, feel excited, feel disappointed, feel fat, feel thin, or feel just right! Whatever feelings flow, they are what they are. Deal with them honestly and do not suppress them. They are a valid and viable part of your journey. Obtain assistance to deal with destructive feelings.

Goal Set – Don't jump into your endeavor "willy-nilly". Prior to beginning your healthy life weight plan, research nutrition information, consult with your physician, and analyze where you are in comparison to where you want to be. Set goals. You do not have to make this a lofty activity accompanied by sub-objectives, and measurement standards. However you do need to identify what success will mean, and how you will know you have achieved it. Chunk your goals into daily, weekly, bi-weekly or monthly intervals to benchmark your progress. You will more easily be able to control and adjust, so that you don't bite off more than is good for you to chew (literally!) The short successes will eventually add up to one *major* one.

Honor Your Spirit – Choose your *inner spirit* as your partner and your "enforcer". Let the spirit, which is you at your best, lead and encourage you. Let your *spirit-of-self* refute any doubt of your ability to succeed. If you have not previously had a *real* relationship with your true spirit-of-self, honor Y-O-U by inviting it into this process.

Invest in YOU! – Come up with any and everything you will need as a down payment...time, money, equipment, medical expertise, a support network, nutrition expertise, workout clothing or a re-stocked pantry/refrigerator. YOU ARE WORTH THE INVESTMENT! I am sure you have wasted monies on things of less importance. You will receive a huge
ROI (return-on-investment) in health and happiness.

Join in with people or activities supportive of your goal(s) – Health clubs and organized weight-loss programs are not for everyone. If you are a person who dislikes groups or organized activities, ask one or two people whose company you enjoy, to exercise with you. You need both the support and accountability of someone else. If you can afford a personal trainer it might be worth your comfort level to employ one.

Kindle Friendships – Initiate friendships with others seeking similar accomplishments. Forging kinship with like-minded people on the same path provides a pallet of support and understanding. You will be able to laugh, commiserate, and encourage each other.

Learn from Mistakes – Learn, not only from your mistakes, but from the mistakes of others. If something does not work for you, or if you slip up on your plan, acknowledge it, correct it and <u>move on</u>. Backsliding is not an excuse to fail. Use the incident as a tool towards strength and endurance.

Mind Your Mind Set – Pay tremendous attention to your mental attitude. Preparation of your mental state is as important as planning your meals and physical exercise. The 'Power of Positive Thinking' is not a joke. Negative thinking can very rapidly destroy a goal. If your modus operandi is positive commitment, your behavior (your body) should follow. Reinforcement of a positive attitude will ground good habits. It must be a deliberate activity. You warm up your muscles prior to exercise, so warm up your mind for to this life changing process.

Navigate through Issues of Impact – Simply put, "it's not about the food!" Over and over again, it has been proven that overeating, eating disorders, and obesity, usually have little to do with love of food, or obsessive compulsion to eat. It is a replacement, "drug of choice", or an exercise in denial to divert attention away from a problem we refuse to acknowledge, accept, and resolve.

Operate From Your Power Base – If you are not certain you can sustain your momentum to successful conclusion, you need to lay a foundation of strength. You will need to feel confident and powerful in your ability to navigate your goals. Learning to meditate and get in touch with your quiet side offers you strength and inner discipline. Getting involved in personal enrichment classes such as self-esteem or positive thinking could be fortifying. Or, you might just want to spend some time journaling. Compile a list of things you like about yourself. Next, list positive things others have said about you, or document successes you have had. Perhaps there is an old resume you can update showing recent accomplishments you have taken for granted. Sometimes we do not realize how much we do, or how talented we are unless we write it down or someone brings it to our attention. If you need a personal lift to feel better about yourself, a new hairdo, a manicure, or spa day might be the ticket. Read something motivational, or volunteer to help someone else. Perform any activities that will help you identify your personal strengths, abilities, and power.

Patience is a Virtue; Praise is Good – I reiterate that changing to a healthy life weight is an evolution. Be patient with your mind, your spirit, *and* your body. Give all components an opportunity to adjust and enter into the new flow. As the little successes begin to materialize feel free to offer praise (personal and/or spiritual). Look in the mirror, admire and hand out an "atta-boy or atta-girl". It is not ego, it is deserved.

Quitting is not an option! – When doubt, fear, depression, or failure, rear their ugly heads do not entertain them. Call on your support system(s) to keep your momentum going. Envision the end result of your goals...see the new you. Do not Quit!!

Restraint, Restraint, Restraint! - Remember how in real estate the mantra is location-location-location? The principal is the same. First, midway, and last, changing just a little will reap huge results. Restrain from more salt, more sugar, and larger portions. The basic skills in this case (3 R's) are restraint, restraint, restraint!

Stay Focused - Keep your eye on the prize. Don't let "friends" obstruct your path. Sometimes others get jealous of your success. Be mindful of your goals on a daily basis and stay in control.

Value the Journey - Feel and see your self as you will be after you have successfully attained your goal. Appreciate each effort along the way.

Wean & **W**ork - Wean yourself of old habits, and environments that are not good for you. Work hard at maintaining a rhythm to your effort.

"X" - You do not want X anywhere in your wardrobe size ... not XL, XXL, 1X or 2X. No "X" marks the spot.

Yearn for the way you want to be - Keep the desire and motivation alive. Post an old photo of you at a smaller size, or display clothing in the size you want to be.

Zest will enhance the experience – Flavor your experience with variety, a positive attitude and gusto. Don't make this drudgery, or it will be all the more difficult to be successful. Develop fun ways to exercise, interesting recipes to delight your palate, and different activities to enrich you in a positive way.

==========

ABCS OF GETTING IT – RELATIONSHIPS

Argue less – to prevent discord
Benevolence - practice it regularly
Comradeship – a reciprocal agreement
Deference – is not demeaning
Enlighten – do not force opinions
Friendship – Frankness; Frivolity
Guidance – Graciously give it
Holistically Exist – take *ALL* of it in
Intrigue – incorporate it
Joy – bring it
Kindness –always a useful tool
Love - abundantly
Mellow and Mindful – the best control
Nurture – for both your sakes
Optimism – shine the light
Patience – the couple's watchword
Quality – a goal worth shooting for
R E S P E C T – speaks for itself
Sensitivity – make it a habit
Trust – a major building block
Unity – without it what is the point
Vitality – set the pace
Willingness – display your generosity
"X" marks the spot - the love environment
Yin/Yang - (passive/active; male/female)
Zeal – bump it up a notch

ABCS OF GETTING IT – RELATIONSHIPS

Argue less - Arguing is not constructive. It usually yields a "lose-lose" result. Evaluate the importance and validity of your stance *before* you argue it.

Benevolence - Practice acts of benevolence as often as possible. Be generous in your tone of voice, in your attitude, with your support, and with your love.

Comradeship – Be a reciprocal companion. Give as well as receive, and honor the friendship that exists.

Deference - is not demeaning – Offer a courteous "right-of-way" when it is meaningful to do so. Occasional yielding is empowering.

Enlighten - don't opinionate – "Share" thoughts, remain open-minded, and welcome two-sided conversation. Listening is also a powerful communication tool.

Friendship/Frankness/Frivolity – Be the best possible friend to your partner. Offer truth, trust, support, compassion, humor, as well as companionship.

Guidance – No one has all of the answers. If you feel the need to offer unsolicited advice, temper it as gentle guidance, rather than an order or act of control.

Holistically Exist – Keep in the forefront of your existence the sum total of what you both bring. No weakness should be *over*-valued at any given time. Enjoy the sex, the looks, the brains, and the earning potential, but accept traits of lesser worth as the basis to appreciate each other's strengths *and* differences

Intrigue - incorporate it. A spike in the daily routine never hurt anyone. Guard against becoming complacent and predictable. Never forget the "curious anticipation" in the early days of your relationship.

Joy - bring it- A little joy goes a long way. Joy can turn sadness into pleasure and lift spirits to unknown heights.
A joyful attitude is a great pallet for positive interaction

Kindness – There is no substitute for kindness to break
down barriers, and overcome anger and sadness.

Love abundantly – The very nature of love carries much power. If you offer it without reservation it will be returned to you exponentially.

Mellow and Mindful – Calmness and thoughtfulness can add positive advantage to situations. Don't be too quick to fire up an attitude. Be mindful of the human trait to misuse those closest to us.

Nurture – Cultivate the atmosphere you want and need in your relationship. For positive growth, you must give care and attention to the "couple".

Optimism – Expect the goodness, the wonder, the integrity, and the understanding. Live and give with optimism.

Patience – Is not only a virtue, it is a necessity. Tolerance, sensitivity, and fortitude make for an enduring journey.

Quality – Simply put, quality will depend upon how well you integrate all of the other Relationship characteristics.

R-E-S-P-E-C-T – You give it to earn it. The watchword is Juxtaposition…"do unto others"… walk in each other's footprints before you act, react, or emote

Sensitivity – Being sensitive is not synonymous with being weak. It is, instead, a clairvoyant instinct; an endearing gift.

Trust – No trust, no value to the relationship!

Unity – Relationships should not negate your individuality; regarding issues for the good of both, exercise unity.

Vitality – Demonstrate "joie de vivre". Bringing joy and positive energy to a relationship can help keep the freshness and verve that often so quickly disappear.

Willingness – Cultivate a spirit of openness. Reserve judgments, "attitude", and negativism.

"X" – Xanadu, the idyllic beautiful haven where you environ your relationship. "X" creates the special space you both create to nurture and safely exist as a couple.

Yin/Yang- The balance between male female is as old as creation. Allow it to maximize your interaction and compliment your existence. Part of coupling is the oppositeness of your personalities and preferences. Revel in the active and passive nature of each other.

Zeal/ Zest - An attitude, an energy, a decided choice of what you want in your relationship environment. Enthusiasm, and passion will probably be more welcomed than apathy and drudgery.

===========

ABCS F GETTING IT – RAISING CHILDREN

Acknowledge children - as "people"
Believe in who they are
Constraints...have them
Deserve to be a parent
Encourage them
Frame their daily existence
Garner their trust
Have faith
Instill confidence
Joy of the **J**ob
Kindle sparks
Love them unconditionally
Mentor them
Need them to be children
Own responsibility for their development
Praise & Punishment
Quiet Security
Remember
Stand on the promise of their future
Trust the gifts
Understanding, understanding, understanding!
Vent on your own time
Waste not want not.
X-Ray vision
Youth...don't envy theirs
Zest and **Z**eal for the children too!

Acknowledge children as people - A pet peeve in my youth was being treated as a "child". I was a child, but that did not mean I was not a human with feelings, needs, and even opinions. Mine certainly were not as developed or as intense as grown ups, but I did have a working mind. Yes, there are differences in appropriateness of events, language, and circumstances that differ for children. However, a child should not be a non-entity from birth through late teens and in the 18th or 21st year they are magically supposed to morph into a functioning adult. Offer information as your children are ready to receive and accept it. Teach them responsibility as they are able to handle it. Be cognizant of their wants and needs and allow them understand and grow in life as a daily learning experience. All children cannot be lumped into a single category. The maturity level and gifts differ with each individual. Honor it!

Believe in them and back them up: Children need support. They are too precious a gift to take lightly. Ensure that you do not bulldoze their self-esteem or their potential simply because you are lazy, angry, jealous, or insecure. Stand up for them, stand behind them, or even stand in front of them as protection when you must. Let them feel secure.

Constraints...You must set boundaries and parameters for both growth and protection. They need to know the impact and the consequences of their behaviors and decisions.

Deserve - the gift of parenting them – Children *are* a gift, and so is parenthood. Parents must honor the commitment required to do their best in raising children. Selfishness, ignorance, mean-spiritedness, inattentiveness, lack of love, and placement in harms way cannot be involved.

Encourage them whenever possible – Champion your children. Allow them the freedom to choose and seek their own way, and give them the tools and support needed to succeed. Participate where you can; cheer them on.

Frame their daily existence. Children need structure, schedules, educational activities, and people they can count on day in and day out, in order to build character.

Garner their trust – Parents and other adults must carry themselves in a way that will offer security to children. Children must

KNOW by what they see from us that we can be counted on for love, honesty, respect for the law, provisions for daily living, and truth.

Have faith – in the child and in your parenting ability. Hone your skills. Prepare and practice. If you make, a mistake regroup and try to do better next time. Have discussions with partners and others who can help you. Know that if you do your best no more can be required.

Instill a sense of confidence. Lay a foundation of values exercising compassion both in teaching and in discipline. Model self-worth so they will emulate you.

Joy on the **Job** – Yes, parenting is a full-time job. Take it seriously, but at the same time don't miss the joy. Savor the many milestones and unmatchable moments it offers.

Kindle sparks that will yield self-worthiness early on. Let your children know they are equal to anyone on the planet. Nurture and reinforce them daily.

Love children unconditionally; it is the best support and gift you can give. They need the security of unrestricted love.

Mentor – At every opportunity, shepherd them to and through life's processes and their aspirations. As parents we must model what we teach. If we do not have our "act together" how much can we require of them?

Need them to be the children they are. Don't try to rush them into adulthood. Monitor that they have age-appropriate activities and entertainment. Clothe them properly for their age, and don't force them to be your friend, equal, companion or parent. Give them time to mature at a healthy pace; convenience for you is not a good enough reason to accelerate that process.

Own your responsibility in their development. Don't leave a child to fend for his/her self. Provide outside stimuli and varied experiences. Don't be a by-stander in their education, get involved. Expose children to multi-ethnic/cultural growth. Shed a positive influence on how they see the world and their place in it.

Praise openly; punish privately. Punish with perspective. Thoroughly think about the reason and the dose prior to issuing punishment. Physical abuse offers no possible positive result. Embarrassing a child in front of people is not effective in correction or connection. Overly punishing will only ensure animosity or timidity. And always temper with love and purpose.

Quiet security – As children grow they need adults to back up a little bit to give them room. Though they need to know we are there, they also need space to breathe, experiment, falter, and recover on their own.

Remember – You were once a child. Don't get amnesia when it comes to giving them understanding. Adults can become very self-righteous with grade-schoolers and teenagers when they step a little out of line. It might serve us well to think back to when were that age, and realize their feelings and dilemmas. Doing so might lend some wisdom to the correct way to proceed. As well as teaching and guiding, we must also relate.

Stand on the promise of the future, but count on what you have invested into your children. Realize that more often than not, you get out of them what you put into raising them. Always there are exceptions to the rule, but pretty much if you lay a solid life foundation at the age a child begins to comprehend, it will pay forward in years to come. Lessons and wisdoms might lie

Words In The Key Of Me

dormant, but when needed will be there to draw upon. Invest your best and results will witness to your efforts.

Trust – Trust your gifts and their gifts. Do the best that you can in reference to both while you have care over them.

Understanding, understanding, understanding! You cannot offer too much. All of us want it…children crave and need it more.

Vent – Vent on your own time when children are not around to see or hear you. Some reaction to certain situations is normal. However, getting overly angry, being obnoxious, using profanity, and exercising melodrama will only set an example which will later come back to haunt you and the world in the worst way.

Waste not, **W**ant not – Figuratively speaking, our children are on loan to us. We must therefore maximize our time and efforts on their behalf…there are no "do-overs!"

X-ray vision – a skill you must acquire in order to penetrate children's souls. You must be able to see and address the hurt, pain, rejection, and confusion they will not share with you.

Youth – Do not envy or be jealous of it. You had your turn, so allow children to exist without competing with you. They don't need you to dress like them and hang out with them and their friends. They need you to be their PARENT.

Zest and **Z**eal - Children deserve to have flavor and enthusiasm added to their lives too. Expose them to new and wonderful experiences in all areas of life. Be excited that you are family to them.

===========

NAVIGATION II – It's Personal

The following expressions are not in order of origin. Some date back 30 years, others are as recent as the last 18 months. Amazingly, my mind is pretty much still in sync with the voice no matter the time...

WHY AM I HERE?

A haunting refrain repeated over and over throughout my existence...since the first time I could comprehend the word "purpose"...

The answer cannot lie only in the coming together of two people for love's sake...it must ensconce more fabric than that

My parents ... simply a conduit, my vessel, my transport, the silage for development of muscle and bones

The substance of my soul comes from a higher source which embraces the mystery of my purpose...it holds captive the key to this burning query

When I was a young thing, I thought I was here to play, and have fun...my spirit then showed me, through experiences, that I was here to learn and grow

But, to what end? Certainly not just for the sake of self. The learning must yield preparation *for* something...but what?

I cannot simply be here to clone someone else via my discoveries; I know too little...I have no <u>real</u> answers

Words In The Key Of Me

No matter what I was shown and taught, lessons were truly learned only through the trials of navigating my own path...ah, some lessons took SO long to learn...

Even though they came at me time and time again, though differently clothed, I often had not eyes to see, nor ears to listen, not mind to give attention to, nor heart to receive... until it was too late...until I was habitually life-embattled

I trod along sometime in glee, sometime in sorrow, and even in numbness... At first, it seemed like a long slow journey then suddenly, I realized the increasing speed of it ...

I was moving faster ... sometimes out of control, and absorbing at a slower pace, or forgetting what I once knew...

Alas, time appears to be running out... But, running out for what? Where is my personal blueprint? How will I find it?

Perhaps, it has been forfeited...I look around...others seem to have found their purpose...some in childhood or young adulthood...some seem to have been multi-purposed...

There are days I feel an inkling of experiencing my purpose, but it is fleeting... and the void returns...

Occasionally in partaking of good times, offering grace, or sharing with a known entity or even a stranger, I feel resolution. I think, "this is what it is all about". But then, dissipation into emptiness yet again...

As I try to latch on and identify an experience as my purpose...and track it back to specific behaviors or activities, it evaporates... just melts away...it eludes me one more time.

Perhaps I fulfilled it unknowingly... for it is God who makes the determination... not we whose lowly interpretations of *His* obedience mean nothing in the real scheme of things. No one ever reaches perfection, but striving for it must continue... I guess until my spirit moves on...

The frustration of it is, I have reached the 6th decade of my existence, and I know the time of my purpose is growing short... The tease is taking its toll, and I am growing weary of this yearning to understand...

THIS CANNOT BE ALL THERE IS...I MUST HAVE BEEN FATED FOR MORE!

I realize and accept that purpose is different for each individual, and that it is not identified by its magnitude, by how much light is shed upon it, or how many people are able to recognize the contributing spirit of it ...However, something inside tells me I am purposed to contribute more to the world...

Have I not been listening intently enough? Have I ignored the signs from my Creator? Am I too lazy and un-ambitious? I am stubborn...has that been my stumbling block? I am shy...should I have tried harder to façade?

What will happen if I don't find this purpose of mine? Will I lose my place of reward in the afterlife venue? Will I be outcast? Will I not partake of the reunions I so look forward to?

It is all too overwhelming... I close my eyes, stay quiet and try to listen, intent upon recognizing the guidance, a map of footsteps, or words of direction that will send me catapulting to it...

Ruth Ann Trent

I *must* be in furious progression toward it, as I am running *so* late... Albeit, if it comes soon, and I fulfill purpose even but for a little while, I know it will be satiating.

Yet again, I wonder...could my purpose have been broken into a gazillion little "partial offerings" that I have been doling out through my attempt to be a good person, a meaningful parent, a faithful spouse, a deserving citizen, a true friend, a decent sibling, a righteous daughter, a God-loving Woman? No, that is too simple and feels as not enough ...

I beg thee Universe, *please* come to my rescue with a sign...lead my being to its path of purpose so that when I depart from *this* place I shall have left my contribution, and I can embark on my new journey in peace!!

THE DECADE OF MY EVOLUTION

A metamorphosis occurred when I was ten
I became different than I was before then
Before 10, my being was never my own
After 10, I could evidence that I had grown

I don't mean in height and weight and face
But my heart and spirit arrived at a special place
My self, for the first time had met the real "Me"
I was forever changed, and I knew it instantly

There was now a perfect fit with my brain and soul
For the very first time I felt completely whole
My walk, my talk, my joy, even my pain
Operating in syncopation, nothing inane

I knew who I was and how I wanted to be
I had no obligation with others to agree
This was MY journey, MY gig, MY path
The consequences were mine at which to laugh

If I screwed up it would be my own decision
Or I could navigate life with boring precision
I was like no one else, my unique life to claim
I embraced it to live through my given name

Ruth Ann Trent

I was fearless to move forward, I knew at age 10
I had become my eternal self forever and within
What a blessing that early bond with my inner voices
It offered me confidence as I made life's choices

ON THE WINGS OF PRAYER

On the wings of prayer, I survived experimenting with things that could have harmed me in my youth, and on the wings of prayer I grew to become a responsible adult

On the wings of prayer I made a poor marriage choice, but I stood by my vows, tried to be the best wife I could be, and on the wings of prayer escaped back into peace and sanity

On the wings of prayer, it only took 10 years to end the active mourning of the death of my Mother; I miss her still, but on the wings of prayer I can cope

On the wings of prayer I survived the difficult journey of never knowing my father's love, and on the wings of prayer my mother was able to successfully parent me anyhow

On the wings of prayer I was vessel to a great spirit coming into this world…he is now a fine man, and on the wings of prayer he will make his positive mark on my grandchildren and this universe

Ruth Ann Trent

On the wings of prayer I survived bad relationships I entered into because I was running from something else, yet on the wings of prayer I have experienced bonds of love and friendship for which there is no description

On the wings of prayer, I was blessed to be among six siblings who are the greatest combination of talent, brains, compassion, and humor to be found anywhere; I am thankful to be able to think, see, smell, hear, speak, and walk... so I clasp my hands together and say a humble "hallelujah"...for the wings of prayer!

MY MARRIAGE

I thought I was in love when I was not even
"in like"
I was in love with the idea of love

I loved the caring, sharing, being needed,
and being desired
I loved the idea of compromising for the good
of two

I wanted to be everything that was missing
from "his" life
I tried to make him whole, and I nearly lost
self and soul

I gave too much and required too little; gave
him my gifts
I never received even the gift of effort in
return

I melted myself trying to become who he
wanted me to be
I absorbed his desires and choices as if they
were my own

I became his strength and had only
weakness left for myself
I witnessed the disappearance of the
essence that was me

Ruth Ann Trent

I believed the vows I recited, but they let me down
I naïvely deposited my love into the wrong account

I came to believe I did not have to live my mistake forever
I am thankful I chose not to punish myself for a lifetime

I am joyfully free
I am again genuinely ME

OUT OF NOWHERE, AN "ANGEL"

After so many years of being half of a couple
After being "Mrs." somebody, or so-and-so's wife
I am alone
I am also free
It is unsettling
It is simultaneously exhilarating

I mourn and I celebrate
I am lost and I am found
I can now spoil _me_
Whew! What a learning curve

I have chosen celibacy
Fidelity is important to me
Therefore I offer it to myself

Someone will eventually motivate me to extricate
Myself from this state
If I accept, the terms will differ from the past

I will want to indulge only in the
Physical excitement of a sexual excursion
I refuse to involve myself in the emotional dance,
The baggage carrying, or the responsibility of a relationship

Ruth Ann Trent

Now, *he* has presented himself
And I don't know how to react
I have been waiting for him
Yet, I am clueless to respond

I *want* him
But find myself unable to articulate my desires…
Suddenly I am speechless
Seven years in hiding have rendered me insecure
I would have thought the *hunger* might
Negate my shyness and lack of confidence

I don't want to be judged
I don't want to be analyzed
I don't want to be scrutinized
I have been happy, independent, and peaceful

I am afraid of what "contact" will mean
I am afraid of its impact on my balance and my future
He has arrived and unleashed the desire
To let go of my revisited virginity

Am I ready to begin again, wrapped in the wings of
An *"Angel"*, and is that "Angel" really ready for me?
I have no desire to be a surrogate
I have no desire to be carried

I wish only to float, in sync, to a meaningful outcome

WITHOUT FATHER

From his photos, he had the kindest eyes...

I use to wonder what it would be like to run and jump into his arms; I hated growing up without a Father
I use to resent that my siblings remembered him and I could not; I loved hearing stories about my Father, his music, and his fabulous personality

I watched my Mother lonely, and alone... parenting five children; I watched her dedicate her life to having no strange man around her daughters; I watched the "quiet rock" that she was, missing the man she had loved; I watched her take on the great responsibility of going on without him

My Father's spirit apparently permeated itself into his children; each of us evidence some part of his talents, physical-ness, or personality; It is amazing how heredity will tell, even without the presence of the flesh; I only hope his spirit continued to stay with and comfort my Mother

I wondered how different holidays would have been had he lived longer; I wondered where and how differently we might have lived; I wondered what life issues might

Words In The Key Of Me

have a different impact, a different outcome;
I wondered if my childhood environment
would have been better or worse

My origin knows him, but I do not; And
though it is the wish I would request from
a genie or fairy godmother, it adds a quiet
joyful curiosity to traveling toward the end
of my earthly life cycle...to that glorious
reunion when our spirits get to meet and
really know each other at last

FIFTY-EIGHT, PLUS ONE

Where have they gone, all those years?
58 of them so swiftly away
Amid many smiles, and many tears
On fleeting feet as if just one day

What an awesome trip
Over 5 decades long
Had to be smart, steadfast,
And had to be really strong

What a short journey
Seems only yesterday
50 years of age
Seemed *so* far away

Would not ever trade it
Not the entire trip, anyhow
Might change a few things
That ran slightly afoul

Love my life, now and back then
Love the family God put me in
Parents didn't stay nearly long enough
Death calling them early made it a little rough

Have no complaints, God's been more than good
Have more blessings than I or anyone should

Family, meaningful work, friends, and health
An abundant life worth more than wealth

Would I like to live 58 more?
Sometimes yes, sometimes not sure
If I stay in the shape I am in today
I would want to live on, but who is to say

Changes have abounded throughout time
People are disrespectful and there is a lot of crime
Seems to be a fear of loving and a fear of caring
Much easier to have vices, anger, and swearing

If I could survive for many more years
And see brotherly love come to bear
No more oppression, no more false fears
Yes, I would definitely want to be here

If there is no change under the rising sun
I will just as soon have my days be done
Yesterday marked my birthday, it was fun
So today, thank God, I made it to 58 years
+1

THE RELATIONSHIP GENE

How strange that the sibling pool in our family is 2 males,
4 females, and both men are still in their marriages...all four women are not

I wonder what influence was transferred through the genes? Or was it environmental...having been reared by a single Mother? Our Mother was single by way of widowhood. No matter the reason, she was no less single with 5 and later, 6 children.

Did the lack of a male image in the household have impact?
Was there no point of reference from which the girls could build relationships? Were there no visual or interactive lessons for them to derive? They are mostly very strong and independent females...did that come into play?

How come the boys were not affected in the same way?
Their marriages are not always perfect, but they persist.
Do women "cut and run" more often (whether they leave or put the spouse out)?
Do men refuse to give up their "lover-caregiver" partnerships so easily?

Do women set higher boundaries and
standards?
Do women need to see and experience the
"couple-ness" of marriage to duplicate it?
When the children come, do the females get
more bogged down in responsibility?
Do the males have more places from which
to derive their relationship role models?

My Mother, having four girls, vowed not
to involve herself in a relationship with a
man until her daughters were grown. She
maintained that vow. I had no problem with
it because I did not want "any old daddy".
But for her sake, I didn't like that she
sacrificed and probably changed forever part
of her life for me.

I do think I looked for characteristics of my
Father in the men I chose, but I definitely
was not looking FOR a father image. I am
strong, stubborn, and deliberate about what
I want. Sometimes I set standards that are
too high for others, and I admit to often
being inflexible and intolerant of what I
perceive as other's imperfections.

I truly believe I ended my marriage for
valid reasons, and I don't plan to repeat
the mistake. There are things I will try,
and know I don't need to try them again.

Ruth Ann Trent

I am not on a relationship diet…just the "legalization" part of it. I guess it is a matter of peace, so Genealogy has nothing do with it after all!

FIGMANTS

I cannot trust a disciple of God
Who fails to "love one another"

I cannot trust a smiling lion
As my head is clinched between his teeth

I cannot trust a stockbroker
Who has rendered me financial distress

I cannot trust a thief in the night
More than my jewels, he has stolen my security

I cannot put trust in an athlete
When he is subsidized through "connections"

I cannot trust a man claiming to love me
Who shares himself with other women!

ODE TO MOTHER

Mothers are a very special breed
They give so much children need

They give their love, time, help, and all
To lift their children whenever they fall

Growing up, sometimes the child resents Mother
For one particular reason or another

A child will rebel to a certain extent
Mother understands; her rules are well meant

She must have standards of how things should be
To a child's mind, her reasoning is difficult to see

As children grow older, it comes to pass
The realization, the awakening...at last

All of Mother's actions, concerns, and care
Were for the child's best interest and welfare

It is hard to verbalize such grateful emotion
That is now felt for Mother's determined devotion

Mother does not look for any reward

Except that the child's life be of balanced accord

No one in the world to your Mother can compare
And losing her to death is too much to bear

Yet there is joy amidst shed tears
of loving memories from past years.

THOUGHTS TO MYSELF

It's good to be alive when love has found you...

It's a miracle to observe the flesh of my womb progressing toward adulthood...

I would rather have to deal with animals than human beings...animals have a great sense of compassion...

People should be able to work during the hours of the day that are best suited to their individual productivity...

Parents need to more often regard their offspring as PEOPLE, instead of just children...

One needs to know and respect self before entering into a relationship with others...

Music and nature walks can more quickly recruit believers in God than can evangelists...

Friendship is often deeper than kinship...

An avid reader has been educated without college and has traveled without boarding a transport

LIFE'S JOURNEY

As strange as it appears to me
It's just the way life seems to be
When it takes an upward bound
It's only a set-up for a let down!

You set your heart, your plans, your ways
For pleasant and smooth sailing days
But for all the efforts and trying
You end up but with tears and crying.

You try to rationalize and understand
You try to cope with the problems at hand
You must dispel the silly notions
of not controlling your own emotions.

What course do you take? What can you do?
How do you lighten life's burdens on you?
All your strength you muster and prod
Until you've nurtured a suitable façade.

But that's what life is all about
One cannot detour from it route
Goodness is inevitably followed by badness
Happiness generally followed by sadness.

Likened to the seasons that make up the year
Some periods are sunny, bright, and clear
Other times are gloomy, cold, and chilly
And life's terrain will often be hilly.

MORE THOUGHTS TO MYSELF
(re: our dysfunction)

To borrow and paraphrase from the "good book"...when I was a child, I spoke as a child, I thought as a child, and I "acted out" as a child. But when I became a "grown-ass woman", I was compelled to bump it up a notch!! And yes, I expect the same from every other adult. The origin of much of the dysfunction in the world is lack of "bumping ourselves up" to adulthood. Too many of us are still acting like children who don't know how to do better. It is NOT acceptable and it is playing havoc on our society. I think that we are the equivalent of T.V. entertainment to life forms on other planets, who must be tuning in on a regular basis gut-laughing at us...i.e.

Adult parents taking care of ADULT CHILDREN

Women bearing multiple out-of-wedlock offspring

Teenagers rearing themselves

Adult employees FEARING their "bosses"

Political leaders who cannot lead themselves/their families

Entertainment that consists of watching other people squirm under embarrassing circumstances

Criminals being allowed to make huge salaries because they can play sports well

Jailbirds being allowed to have more luxuries than law abiding citizens and their victims

Children dressed as adults parading in "beauty" contests
Family members treating each other like strangers...and strangers being easily able to regularly abduct people

Monthly utilities costing more than home mortgages

Students lack of basic skills in high school, and the fix...more tests and requirements

One human thinking/feeling they are better than another

Teaching our young to hate/destroy versus love/beautify

Expecting that someone or some agency is responsible to take care of our needs

Thinking one has the right to physically abuse another living thing

Feeling entitled to scam any sucker you can find

Working most of your life and having nil to show for it

The masses being led and controlled by the few

Blindly being led by a person-of-the-cloth, just because they claim divine messenger status

Thinking that "different" is synonymous with either better or worse

Not ever experiencing the joy of giving of self

GIVE ME STRENGTH LORD

Give me strength, Lord
Amidst this world of confusion
To do the things I ought
And not fall to disillusion

Give me strength, Lord
Thru times I cannot see
Turn me around point me right
And be a beacon unto me

Give me strength, Lord
When I falter or fall
To regain my balance
And to the feat stand tall

Give me strength, Lord
When I know not where to turn
Send my way someone of wisdom
From whom my humble mind can learn

Give me strength, Lord
In persevering day by day
To be steadfast, to keep the faith
And know you will make a way

Give me strength, Lord
When at an increasing rate
I find I cannot stop the tide
Of love becoming hate

Ruth Ann Trent

Give me strength, Lord
I am not too proud to seek
Even difficult solutions
To mend me where I am weak

A TRUE GIFT OF LOVE

I open my eyes sometimes to darkness,
I open my eyes, sometimes to light
I open my eyes sometimes to rain
I open my eyes sometimes to sun-bright

I see colors I see objects,
I see textures I see shapes
I see the splendor of the day
I see magnificent landscapes

I feel the wisp of the breeze
I feel the rhythm of the trees
I hear the birds in song
I hear the brooks flow along

I view the mountains in majesty
I view the vastness of the sea
I view tree leaves burst in full flare
I view the clearness of pristine air

I watch insects as they toil
I watch flowers burst through soil
I watch animals graze the meadow
I watch forest creatures come and go

Eyes to see, ears to hear
the magnanimous gifts are clear
Sent by the Creator from above
Nature and senses...what LOVE!

MINDSET

Being more positive can actually make us feel better. The mind can lead the body to follow what is inherently good for it. We make life much more difficult and complicated than it ever need be. We work harder at making ourselves uncomfortable and miserable than we do at making ourselves happy.

Who knows why we derive comfort in agonizing, complaining, and being depressed. We also get pleasure by having everyone else around us either experience the misery, or hear about it. What sense does that make? And why is it so difficult to alter?
Why do we enjoy overindulgence? Why do we enjoy pain? Why do we enjoy doing what we know to be harmful to ourselves?

Our origin does not dictate such scenarios. If we followed the will of our intention we would have great lives and attitudes. We were designed to function at the highest level and with the greatest quality. Yet, we choose to sabotage our own existence.

There is something about martyrdom and struggling that becomes addictive. Negative reinforcement is a powerful force!

HOW DO YOU FEEL, LORD?

Do you still marvel, Lord, at the trees when they burst from briery twigs into tender buds and then into floating leaves? Or, are you too saddened to see below them, people fighting.

Do you still marvel, Lord, at the sky...one day billowed with cotton-like clouds, one day amber with solar sparkle, and one day dripping with tender shower drops? Or, are you too sadden by tearful young children being abused by sinful adults?

Do you still marvel, Lord, at the sweet fragrance of the flowers and the sweet nectar of fruits? Or, are you too saddened by the garbage in the waterways, and noxious fumes in the air?

Do you still marvel, Lord, at your miracle of reproduction...be it the birth of a human baby or a furry little puppy? Or, are you too saddened by the abuse to humans and animals through alcohol, drugs, and additives?

Do you still marvel, Lord at the brilliance of the human mind in medicine, technology, the humanities and the arts? Or, are you too saddened by the devious acts of embezzlement and disrespect for one another?

Do you still marvel, Lord that you gave your Son *to* and *for* us? Or are you too saddened to see that we cannot live in peace and brotherhood together?

WHY

Behaving irresponsibly can be so harmful...
As much to ourselves as to anyone else
It is double pain when we hurt someone
else...because, in retrospect, it diminishes
us as well

Many times, there is nothing we can do
to reverse the action or pain...one cannot
erase mental anguish, *ever!* One might
pretend to forget, but it takes its toll on
heart, soul, mind, and body

Why do we anger so quickly?
Why so much insensitivity?
Why are our feelings so brittle?
Why do we feel put upon so quickly?
Why do we not assume the best in others?
Why are we so selfish?
Why are we so competitive?
Why are we so critical?
Why are we are we so mean-spirited?
Fear and insecurity, from where does it
come?

FEELINGS ...

Music:

If I had to choose between going a week without food, or going without music, I would choose to let food go. I cannot imagine a day without music let alone a world without it. There are so many levels from which it speaks to one. I whistle or hum, and I don't realize it until someone tells me that I am doing so.

Our family has always been musical (Thank God!). Mother and Daddy both had beautiful singing voices. Dad also played a "mean" piano. All of us children sang and played musical instruments. My first memories of music were probably of hymns in church. That, perhaps, was preceded by a lull-a-bye sung by parents or siblings. There would be the toddler songs taught in Kindergarten about Old McDonald, and the Itsy Bitsy Spider. As a child at play would come the songs that accompanied jumping rope... those catchy little ditties...i.e. *'Old Mary Mack, Mack, Mack, all dressed in black, black, black, with silver buttons, buttons, buttons, all down her back, back, back. She jumped so high, high, high, that she touched the sky, sky, sky, and she didn't come back, back, back, 'til the fourth of July, ly, ly'.* And later came via the radio, Nat King Cole singing Mona Lisa, or Perry Como, the Andrews Sisters, Mahalia Jackson, Marion Anderson, Clara Ward, the 5 Blind Boys, Roy Rogers and Dale Evans, Mario Lanza, Skitch Henderson, the Boston Pops, and the New York Philharmonic Orchestra. Somebody sang <u>Tweedly Dee - Tweedly Dum</u>, Dinah sang <u>What a Difference a Day Makes</u>, and Frankie sang <u>Lucky Old Sun</u>. Later, James Brown, Elvis Presley, Gladys and the Pips, Stevie Wonder, The 'Temps' and The 'Tops' and an entire different genre of musicians came along and made it even better!

I sang in the church choir at the age of 4...my 8-year-old sister was the choir director and organist. Even though we were the "Baby Choir", we could out sing the birds in the trees. Every time our church visited other churches for musical concerts, we would bring the house down. My brother and me, and neighbor children made up the choir. And my sister did not take any stuff. We sang good harmony or else! She and my older siblings also sang in a trio accompanied by a guitarist and the piano. Either of my two piano-playing sisters did the honors. The thing was, we had excellent pitch, rhythm, and harmony. Different than most folks, and it was God-given and heredity driven. It couldn't quite be duplicated, and it certainly could not be taken away but by God. The crux of music to me is that it is another of God's expression of beauty through mankind. The first time I heard a pop group (Boyz 2 Men) singing a song entitled <u>End of the Road</u>, I had to pull my car over to the side of the road before I had an accident. They hit a chord in that song that just made me scream with sheer glory. I sat there with goose bumps from the beauty I was hearing in note combinations the likes of which could only speak to the magnificence of God. I later found out that many others had reacted in much the same way to their rendition of that song. It was the same as when I heard <u>Amazing Grace</u> being played by Macy O. Woods, or my nephew Scott playing <u>I Love the Lord</u>! I have felt the same sensation listening to Wagner's <u>Die Meistersinger</u>, and countless other songs whether by Boney James or Ray Charles... (what you say!!) Music is all around us whether in the wind blowing the trees, the birds singing, raindrops keeping a beat, or the musical sound of children's laughter.

I keep CDs running through my computer while I am a work and through the player in my car. I book mark Jazz, Gospel, Classical, Country, Opera, and Rock

stations on my car radio. I would truly
rather lose a limb, than lose that pulse of
life and that connection to God's beauty.
In Black church congregations, we have
an expression that people "get happy".
Meaning they feel the Holy Spirit in their
being, and just cannot keep from dancing,
shouting out, crying, speaking in tongues,
clapping hands, or all of the above. The
spirit of music impacts much the same way.
It can make you get happy!

I *do* have a personal differentiation between
what is *real* music and what I deem to be
a lot of noise being passed off as music. I
guess, however, *good* music *is* in the *ear* of
the beholder ...

GIVING BIRTH

I'll try many things once. I firmly believe
it would be great if every woman could
experience bearing a child at least one time.
I happen to be one who did not feel the need
to duplicate the experience. I guess I felt the
mold was broken when I had my wonderful
son Kenneth; he was my only pregnancy.
For a while I felt bad. Since I so enjoyed
my siblings I thought it unfair that he have
none. I opted, instead, to let him spend a lot
of time with his cousins and other children.
That turned out to be a lot easier on me.

Talk about your miracles. The fact that our female bodies can expand to accommodate a fetus, and our system feeds and lubricates its growth with blood and nutrients. Unfortunately, we can also transmit our poisons to it as well. The ability to carry out the reproduction process could only be designed by our Omnipotent Father. I do not care what kind of cloning processes research brings about, the miracle of birth belongs to God. It is wonderful to touch a pregnant woman's stomach, or to feel the movement of the fetus inside of your own body. Even though you gain weight, (sometimes a whole lot of weight) it is not the same as just gaining weight from overeating. You know a miracle is happening with that growth, and it just isn't the same. When you gain weight from overeating, your face looks bloated and you get saggy. With the birth miracle, you get round, firm, and you glow. The really amazing part is the fact that 5 to 12+ pounds of flesh with appendages can come out of that little aperture. The stretching of the stomach is one thing, but this...PLEASE!

Aside from the vessel portion of childbearing, the bond that develops between mother and child is incredible, and if you breastfeed, it only increases. I felt like superwoman when I delivered. I had a natural childbirth, though it was not planned to happen that way. I was totally shocked that I could bear that much pain and not *really* mind. You see we are talking about someone who is middle age, and is STILL petrified of getting a blood draw. We are talking about someone who physically feels pain when it is inflicted upon someone on T.V. We are talking about someone who could not hold her pet at the vets to get its temp taken. So for me to see child birth as a bearable event, and enduring what is certainly the most unbelievable pain on Earth, yet not really carrying on, or minding it...that is a biggy! I just wish everyone could experience it once...even Men!

PETS (ANIMALS)

Some folks get offended if you do not give proper "respect" to their four-legged, two-winged, or two-finned family members. There is a degree to which I can understand that. On the other hand, I think there should be some line between pets and people.

Dogs are my pet of preference. I do have an aversion to vicious-type attack-breed dogs, especially if I do not know them personally. But, for the most part, I think dogs are just the greatest thing since sweet potato pie. I have had Yorkies, Lhasas, Pekes, Malteses, Bouviers, Old English Sheep, and mixed mutts. Dogs are such a loving presence to have in your home, and you don't have to do much to receive the love. When you look up the word *loyal* in the dictionary...Mr. Webster should have just placed a picture of a dog there. So different are they from cats...who are incessantly aloof, stuck up, moody, finicky, and on and on with the snotty personality traits, and jealousy to a vengeance. Dogs get jealous, but they do not retaliate quite like felines. I have never seen a cat defend you like a canine will. Fish...boring...they could not care less about you as long as they get their few little flakes per day. Gerbils and hamsters are too rat-like for me. I could not abide a pet that made me uncomfortable in my own home.

All of my dogs knew my moods. They knew when to comfort, and when to drag me to play. They were pretty patient, understanding, loving and protective of me...even the 5 lb ones. Dogs are pretty low maintenance unless you need to board them often. You have to give it to cats on that score. A little food and water, and cats don't care if you are around or not. I have had my share of birds (not by choice) and they can be pretty choosy as to whom they

Words In The Key Of Me

do or do not like; the more exotic the more "attitude". The ones that speak, *understand* the bad words, and when to come out with an embarrassing phrase. Birds can be quite messy. Turtles are the best, and totally have their act together. They go along at their own pace, bobbing their little heads, shrinking into their shell whenever they please. Now there is a life-style I could embrace.

MONEY

Money is definitely *not* the root of all evil. Evil folks just should not have money! If I inherited a windfall of dough right now, I am certain it would not make me evil. Actually, it might improve my attitude. Certainly if I came into a large sum of money, I would share. There is only so much money a person can spend in a lifetime. And in my humble opinion, money is one thing that should be shared as often as possible by those who have it in abundance. Even though I am not rich, I love sharing my money when I can afford to.

If I worked at the Mint that would pretty much be like working in a chocolate factory. After being around it and seeing it all day, I might just get tired of it. I wonder if many of the very wealthy really share that much of their total holdings. A monetary fortune would make me feel empowered to help others, not to have power over them. If I became wealthy, I would donate to my church, divvy up with my family and close friends, and then seek other opportunities to be charitable. Each family member would not get the same amount, because that is my truth. I would give according to the rules of Ruth, and only my formula would apply. One thing I would like to do is begin a music project to have my family record an album. Anyone who is remotely related to us can be in the mass choir. We would record a gospel album featuring all of the individual talent of voice and instruments. Siblings, children, grandchildren, in-laws ...what fun! And to celebrate its completion, we would all take a trip to Africa, my Motherland. After the initial gospel album, we might do other kinds of secular recordings.

I also want very much to do projects involving education, empowerment and assistance women who need a boost for whatever reasons in their lives.

Health issues would be a great cause to address. I would probably spend just as much money trying to make the government do what is right by citizens, as paying for research. So, as far as coming into a fortune …bring it on, I'll be ready.

NAVIGATION III – The Children

As each generation passes, it seems children become more complicated. Actually, it is not the children, it's the influence of the changing world *on* them and the added pressures parents encounter in their responsibility to shepherd them into adulthood.

Parenting can be pretty scary sometimes, especially if you are a single parent. Children, though they can be difficult to live with, more often give immeasurable and infinitesimal fun, pride, and joy.

A CHILD

To have a child is a wonderful thing
There is limit to the joy it can bring
Not just the good, but when they're naughty too
You have to thank God for that "little you"

To see in them so many of your ways
To watch them grow throughout the days
To nourish, clothe them, and be their guide
To instill in them the meaning of pride

To kiss their little hands when they have a scratch
Or for a big hurt, to place on a patch
To teach them to pray before they sleep
The Lord their little souls to keep

To see their transition into man or womanhood
To know that you've done for them all that you could
To not interfere when they leave the nest
To wish them well and pray for the best

To rear a child is not an easy chore
It takes love, care, time, money, and more
But sacrifices are not too much to afford
For so much greater is the reward

Ruth Ann Trent

The creation of a child is a miracle in itself
Its worth outshines any other form of wealth
For when your time on Earth is through
You've left behind a precious part of you!
(Ken Avery)

I HAVE FEARS

While traveling through my formative years
I invariably had many, many, fears

On Christmas Eve, I feared I would get no toys
On Good Friday, I prayed for Easter joys

I'd become angelic before Thanksgiving came
So I would not be punished for the big football game

The Gods be praised, I made it through
With minimal scars and lots of fun too

My childhood days are past and gone
And now I nurture my child along

A new kind of fear has overtaken me
It is a fear I must take seriously

The fear is for the "now" generation
Their actions in my day rendered degradation

I fear because my child's generation has little hope
I fear for a generation getting false courage from dope

Ruth Ann Trent

I fear for our advice they do not hear
I fear for their lack of goals...they do not care

I have fear when I realize how many youths are jailed
I have fear when I see how many parents have failed

I have fear when I see strain in family after family
I have fear seeing the decline of our society

I have fear for our children's future state
What can I do about these fears I contemplate??

DEAR CHILDREN
(For Ken, Scott, & Guy)

I sat last night for a long time thinking about you and your future. I have tried to answer your questions about life, death, or anything you had on your mind. I took care not to tell you too much for your comprehension, but enough for your satisfaction. The thoughts I had last night were of things you have not yet asked, and things you will not necessarily be able to control, but things by which you will be affected.

I am speaking of crime, war, homosexuality, bigotry, discrimination, and the political drudgery of our society. Not that any of this is new to the human race...just gander through the history books for prime examples.

The thing is, we are now living through it and our present societal attitude is apathetic, and "I don't give a damn!" That frightens me a lot. No one seems to care how they treat others or even themselves. It is the day of the "rip-off". I cannot judge every incident, because who is to determine the root cause of a crime committed or a life of homosexuality.

I was thinking that I do not want my children affected by all of this. I know you are aware of many things, even though you may not have a total understanding. On the other hand, I do not want you to be oblivious, either.

How can you deal with something if you have no knowledge of it? There is not much in life that you will not encounter even if only to know its definition. I could, of course, shield you from any knowledge of drugs, alcoholism, treatment (or mistreatment) in mental and correctional institutions, etc., but you would not be helped one iota by that...it would be unfair.
I could lead you to believe that people rarely steal, kill, and harm innocent victims. Or, I could pretend that our political system does not deal in dishonesty...but that would not be true. I say I could TRY to do this. Undoubtedly you would find out things on your own, and perhaps painfully too late! I remind myself that my mother did not teach me about sex, but I indulged like a masterful "pro", and what I did not know, I soon found out...as will you.

So, dear children, let me say that there will be many things that come up in your lives that will affect you directly, and some things that you will view from a distance. They will sometimes be distasteful and other times shake your beliefs to the very core. These incidents might rally you to take a stand. Whenever they arise, know that I will still be available to answer your questions, or to discuss your thoughts and feelings. Perhaps, together, we can come up with a solution to help you cope with, change, accept, or even reject these different aspects of the world in which we live.

I can pray for your good judgment and teach you what I know is right. And hopefully you will make it through without too much trauma and disillusion. And hopefully too, you will have something to fall back on when the night comes that you find yourself sitting and worrying about your own children.

Lovingly, Ruth Ann Trent, alias...Mom/Aunt Ruthie 1975

HEARTBREAK

If only we could light a torch
And show you, son the way
If only we could grab your hand
And guide you through each day

If only we could let you know
That though there may be strife
You must go on, and try to cope
For that's the choice in life

It isn't always easy
It's rarely ever fun
To try to figure out what's right
To stay out from under the gun

These "things" that you're supposed to do
Don't seem too appetizing
You feel they're hard, not right for you
I find that not surprising

We parents who dish out this advice
Don't understand your generation
But we keep right on butting into your life
To your very consternation

It's not your fault there is no work
Quite suitable for you
That seems to be the convenient excuse
You choose to pretend is true

Words In The Key Of Me

School was boring, a real drag
They didn't motivate you there
And now without an education
You cannot get anywhere

Why don't you stop kidding your self
Be honest just this one time
And admit your tricks and lying
Only present a more difficult climb

All these "smarts" you supposedly have
So you don't have to listen to anyone
Have gotten you no where at no time
And your life just isn't much fun

You know that you are sincerely loved
Though you try to ignore that fact
But it will keep on chasing you
So you might as well clean up your act

We will always be your family
No matter what you become
But you will have to face *your self*
When all is said and done

A LETTER TO DAVID

My dear "nephew" David (Son of my friend Lillian)

I am sending you some words of wisdom and encouragement, as well as some reminders. Your mother and I talk, and of course the subject of our sons comes up. I hope you are well, and moving forward with your life. I just want to remind you that at this stage of trials and establishment of life you must hold on, because it will eventually yield to success and happiness.

David, you are a talented and blessed young person. Blessed because I know your mother and knew your grandmother and I can witness the goodness from which you come. I did not know your father well, but I know God gives talent and good traits to all, and both parents pass their good genes along to their children. Thus, another positive source of the strength that is inside of you. I know for a fact that as a young child you could sing, dance, learn quickly and you were very formidable at charisma and confidence. That must still be a part of you. If you are not calling upon it, dig it up!

Don't let the world, love, and economics jade your dreams. A little bit of God is in

all of us, which makes you a descendant
of royalty in the highest order. Always
remember that you are special and talented,
and
you deserve only the best. DO NOT SETTLE
FOR LESS.

If you continue to seek to be the best
person, performer, friend, son, and partner
you can be, the universe will lead you to a
love that will make any lost loves laughable.
When the down days or low feelings begin
to overtake you, treat yourself to something
pleasant, or take yourself into the company
of friends, family or acquaintances who will
love and respect you for the great person
that you are. Don't waste a New York
minute on people, activities or thoughts,
that don't honor DAVID! And, when
everything falls into place, it will be just
in time and more satiating than you could
have anticipated. Positively prepare to
receive, for it is on the way.

Love to you,
Aunt Ruthie

COCAINE

Why are our children dying...dying day by day?
Why are our children dying in such a horrific way?
The innocence of our youth will never be the same
And it is adults who are to blame for...
Cocaine

Kids don't plant the seed
Kids don't grow the weed
Kids don't sell the stuff, and someone older must teach them to puff, and sniff, and snort, and shoot and lose everything to ...
Cocaine

Why is it any different than sticking a gun to your head? Will you come back to life? Will you be any less dead?
Why don't we call it suicide...because intent was not there? Our children still kill themselves traveling in the fast lane...
Cocaine

The rich think it is stylish, the "in" thing to do
If you are free and over 21...the choice is up to you
Once that poison hits society, it all becomes a shame

At parties, serving it up, pretending using is a game
but the high is too pricey, and the price is too high
trading a life for...Cocaine

They sell it to the poor, lace it to put the price in range
They sell it to our seniors for their Social Security change They give it to our collegiate as a reward for their success They give it to our pregnant moms...babies are born a mess
It is insane, this *killer*...Cocaine

EVELYN LORENA AND HER CREDIT

I'm in so much trouble, how can I face my mother?
She will fuss, she will fret...have one fit after another
No need to stand here trembling, overcome with fright
I might as well go tell her what I got into tonight

I sauntered into the Lady Bug to look for some pants
I didn't think I'd find anything, but still I took a chance
Looking around at all the clothes, gazing nonchalantly
a clerk approached to ask if she could be of help to me

I turned around and gave her a look that was funny
I forced myself to confess to her that I had no money
She said that shouldn't cause me a problem for today
If I did not have the cash, I could put it on lay-a-way

If that plan didn't suit me, if waiting was to hard

Words In The Key Of Me

I could instantly apply for their in-store credit card
I would take clothes, and bill them to a charge plate
And not even have to pay for them until a future date

One little problem if my payments should be late
The store will add interest at a set percentage rate
I was suddenly so happy I almost did a dance
I could shop and shop and chalk it up to finance

I bought lots of clothes and shopped for over an hour
I filled my heart's desire to test my purchase power
I had skirts, pants, so much I could not believe
I was having so much fun I did not want to leave

I had to stop shopping…I was the last one in the store
My arms were so tired, and I could not hold anymore
I went up to the cashier for her to get a figure count

Ruth Ann Trent

And I was really stunned at the huge total amount

The register clicked and stopped at a hundred dollars
I knew when I got home my Mom was going to holler
I didn't mean to buy so much I got carried away
Now what am I going to do when it comes time to pay

I guess I now know the bitter-sweet taste of credit
I had a ball, I am well dressed, and I don't regret it!

(Rena & Aunt Ruthie – for a class assignment)

NAVIGATION IV – Oh, It MUST be Love!

MY CHANGE HAS COME

I thought I lived, I thought I loved
I thought my life was set
I thought things had to be one way
Until the day we met

I soon found out how life could be
So gloriously that day
You blew my mind and captured my heart
In such a gentle way

Your total being stays with me
No matter what I do
I kneel down and thank the Lord
That he has sent me you

Short time was spent in finding out
That we matched perfectly
I kneel again to thank the Lord
That he has sent you me

Now we plan our lives anew
For body, mind, and heart
A life of love and togetherness
With hope to never part

SPRING IN DECEMBER

It matters not a bit to me
Whether they think I am silly
I love him so my mind is hazy
Yet everyone whispers that I am crazy

It's the sweetest love I've ever known
I feel young again, and not alone
So what's the difference, why all the rage
Because the man is half my age

I have the right to make my choice
And in my decision I rejoice
So love I will with utmost haste
I've not been promised life to waste

He may change and want to go
Find someone younger, I don't know
But with that fear I will have to live
For now, I'll take what he will give

Just let them talk and point and stare
People can laugh I do not care
One day I'll fondly look back and remember
My young love...my Spring in December

(Lois and Ronnie)

LOVING HIM IS...

Making him the focal point of my life
Being number two in his life and mine
Wanting to be with him at any given moment
Wanting to be near something of his when he is away
Wanting to bear his child
Freely giving him my body and soul
Keeping his ego accelerated
Always being there when he needs or wants me
Not complaining about his double standards
Remembering all the special occasions in his life
Helping him achieve what he desires to be
Being the first to apologize even when I am right
Saying "yes" when he wants to and I don't
Not being unfaithful even though he has been
Being tactful when criticizing him
Loving the way he walks and talks

Authors note: (that was back in my "pitiful" days!)

LOVE SICK

I love your eyes as they reflect the love you see in me

I love your arms because they hold me with the strength of your passion

I love your hands because they tenderly transmit a non-verbal message of love

I love your lips because they taste and tell the feelings of your heart

I love your legs for the very leverage they give when you mount me

I love your torso to which I can cling while on my sexual excursion

I love your mind with which you think out your considerateness

I love you "in toto" because there is so much about you to love

WHEN YOU FIND THAT MAN

When you think you're in love
And have the perfect man
You'll put your best foot forward
And do for him all that you can

You'll not only feed him
You will clothe him too
You'll sweat blood and tears
To have him pleased with you

You'll spend your money
To make yourself pretty
And whenever he is near
You'll "purr" like a kitty

Anything he says
Will be just right
You'll give total attention
And show great delight

You'll keep him feeling
Like he is a king
And in bed with him
You'll really do your thing

You'll give him tender care
When he is feeling bad
You'll try to cheer him
When he is feeling sad

From time to time
You'll squeeze him tight
You'll tell him you love him
With all your might

So now that you've found
That grown up little boy
No need to try to be
Reserved and coy

Even if you start out
Being calm and cool
For that man of yours
You'll be a loving fool

WE CAN

Why can't you just love me
Why do we have to disagree
I love you so sincerely, don't you see

How come you cannot trust me too
As you expect my trust in you
It's something we must do to see this through

I know just where the problem lies
I see it in your eyes
The fear of losing our love ties

Hold onto me so
As if you dare not let me go
There's no one else, that you know

We must stop wasting time my dear
I cannot be any more sincere
I want you with me here...so near

Just for once let us be smart
Fulfilled anew we will start
Let's follow our heart

As long as we shall live
No matter what the challenge is
We must swear to each other to forgive

MY VALENTINE

I love my valentine because...
Just thinking of him makes my heart race
And brings an unstoppable smile to my face

When there are times we disagree
It's refreshing that he is the opposite of me
Yet, on important things about which I think
Our beliefs and hearts are likely in sync

His eyes reflect the love he sees in me
His arms hold me with security
He's kind, compassionate, and very dear
Life is sweet when he is near

His mind thinks about what is best
I know through him I am truly blessed
His heart is mountain high and wide as the sea
My valentine is the absolute best gift for me

(a contest...took 2nd place)

MY BAHAMA BABY

Eyes as deep as the ocean
A smile as wide as the sea
My Bahama Baby
Touched a cord in me

A velvet voice to soothe you
A heart pretending to be true
My Bahama Baby
Made me feel brand new

He was so sweet and gentle
As handsome as can be
My Bahama Baby
Brought such joy to me

Memories of balmy days
Warm evenings all aglow
My sweet Bahama Baby
Just what I needed, don't you know!

(the "Stella" experience)

IT'S POSSIBLE

To really hurt and not cry
Is impossible
To live and not die
Is impossible

To grow and not learn
Is impossible
To think and not discern
Is impossible

To feel and not experience pain
Is Impossible
To progress and never gain
Is impossible

To give and never take
Is impossible
To lie and not be fake
Is impossible

To try and never win
Is impossible
To exist and never sin
Is impossible

So what is left to do
That will be possible
To put my trust in you
Is possible

NAVIGATION V – The Love Is Gone!

WHEN IT IS OVER

No one can say why things happen as they do
No one can say why we get so low and blue
Where once there was happiness and all rejoiced
There is now sadness and you mourn alone

No one can explain what is right or wrong
No one can ensure that you can be strong
Where once there was comfort and care
There is now uncertainty and anger

No one can predict what your future will be
No one can answer for your destiny
Where once you had direction and purpose
There is now indecision and vulnerability

There is no one to soften this burden you bear
There is no way to magically remove your fear
Where once you felt special and confident
There is now emptiness and insecurity

There is no one to answer what will become of your life
There is no way to know if you will survive this strife
Where once you felt tomorrow unshakable
There is now need to walk forward on faith

There is no one who can turn back the
hands of time
There is no one to retrieve the union once
sublime
Where you had the illusion of a relationship
There is now loss and a broken heart
(Dina)

DYING LOVE

Love is leaving me
I don't know what to do
I can't believe how short the stay
I shan't believe it's through

The books, the poems, the fairy tales
All paint love's picture bright
But it has taken in reality
The form of a dimming light

The beginning was so beautiful
So perfect and so gay
Yet now has come a nightmare
Of my love waning away

I feel within my sinking heart
There's got to be some hope
I keep afloat with arms outstretched
But no one throws a rope

I cannot hold on much longer
To something that isn't there
Love has become an outfit
Which I can no longer wear

I shall however clothe my heart
In a suit of armored steel
So if in the future love attacks
Its pain I shall not feel

JUST SO YOU KNOW

Just so you know, my former dear
All those times you were being cavalier
Have boomeranged right back to you
It's payback time for not being true

Just so you know, you took my trust
And you dismissed it as less than dust
But I stood firm and held you high
I was such a fool, I don't know why

Just so you know I am stronger than ever
And this is one storm I will surely weather
My head and heart will definitely bounce back
And my love dreams will still be in tact

Just so you know, you didn't break my spirit
You have no triumph I want you to hear it
That love trauma just made me grow
Just so you know...JUST SO YOU KNOW!

TIRED

I am tired of trying
Tired of crying
Tired of being misused
And tired of being emotionally abused

I'm tired of being distressed
Tired of being depressed
Tired of not being believed
And tired of being deceived

I'm tired of giving with no return
Tired of fighting fires and getting burned
Tired of strain
And tired of pain

I'm tired of tears
Tired of fears
Tired of confusion
And tired of disillusion

I'm tired of madness
Tired of sadness
Tired of false yes's and false no's
And tired of not knowing which way to go

And of course, I AM TIRED OF BEING TIRED!

APOLOGIES

I apologize for loving you
I apologize for accepting the things you do
I apologize for your jealousy
I apologize for your unjust treatment of me

I apologize for handling you as a precious jewel
I apologize for being your footstool
I apologize for caring for you
I apologize for wanting to be cared for too

I apologize for holding on and even trying
I apologize for my late-night crying
I apologize for not putting up a defense
I apologize for your lack of sense

I apologize for letting you run my life
I apologize for becoming your wife
I apologize for letting you to bring me pain
I apologize for letting you make my life a game

I apologize for an affirmative instead of a "no"
I apologize for not forcing you to go
I apologize for the last time...now I am through
And, I apologize to ME baby, not to you!!

PLAYING THE WHEEL OF LOVE

I was once a gambler
I played the odds and lost
I placed my chips on a thing called love
But I could not cover the cost

The wheel of love spun around
My heart was set for its stop
It slowly unwound, came to a halt
I saw I was not on top

My ego being what it was
I gave it a try again
A second time love's wheel spun down
Once more I did not win

The tension built within me
As the wheel turned and rattled out
Each click whispering a challenge
For me to persist in the bout

I slowly wiped my chips away
Couldn't stand another try
I cowered out on the game of love
The stakes were just too high!

TRUST

What happens to trust?
    It is taken for granted

What happens to trust?
    It is violated

What happens to trust?
    We forget its meaning

What happens to trust?
    We trade it without thinking

What happens to trust?
    We don't understand its worth

What happens to trust?
    We think it for the *other person*

What happens to trust?
    We appreciate it when it is too late!

NAVIGATION VI – Pot Pourri

STRESS

I AM *stress*. We *really* need no introduction. You have known me a long time, but may not have realized how long ago we met and how often we have interacted. Perhaps, you just don't always recognize me. I, like participants in a costume ball, disguise my true identity, unless you have caught on to me, or picked up the knack of knowing my revealing characteristics.

I sometimes come dressed in very heavy iron-like attire, pounding away at your cranial membranes. That is my migraine outfit. I possess tremendous staying power; I can last for what seems like forever! I then change into a tight little suit, and squeeze tighter, and tighter. That is my pinched nerve get-up, so I can reach many points in your body...I am very versatile.
I am also aerobically inclined. I can do all sorts of flip- flops in your stomach...on and off, on and off until I am dizzy and you are doubled over in pain. I can also play the dart game...in and out of your rib cage around your heart making breathing and pulse erratic. When I tire of all that, I just make myself very rigid and drip, drip, down, down, down, to the lower spine and lumbar region. There I plop myself on a muscle and just sit until I drive it into shock

and spasm. You might get caught in the
wrong position when I land. If so, too bad,
it will take awhile before you can undo me
when I am in that mode.

When all else fails, I get intellectual. You
know,
I play mind games. I help you retain all the
negative things that are going on around
you. If you try to forget, I bring them right
back to the front of your mind. I hum songs
of woe into your head all day long so that
you can maintain a dark posture. I plant
little suggestions into your psyche about the
people in your life. I am very persuasive,
and you tend to believe the things I tell you.
I keep squeezing those tear ducts (a good
cry never hurt anyone!) I force you to cry
even when there is no reason.

As you look in the mirror at yourself, I
help you see *all* of your flaws very clearly.
If there is something you did not notice, I
helpfully point it out to you. So, you see,
we really need no introduction...we've been
acquaintances for a long, long time. Only,
I identified you early on and you did not
acknowledge my existence or realize my
powers and influence.

So what is our relationship going to be
now that you know of me? What could

you possibly do to change our manner of interaction? You must realize that I am in control! Let's brainstorm a moment... maybe you could do some kind of physical exercise...something enjoyable that doesn't feel like a chore. Perhaps exercise will give you more energy, take your mind off negative things, improve your metabolism, burn off some stress-related calories, tone your body, make you look better, and raise your self-esteem. Or, perhaps you might take a few minutes each day as "quiet time"...steal away to a secret place or just stop wherever you are and close your eyes and think pleasant thoughts or listen to soothing music. You might place a cold compress over your eyes, daydream, read a good poem, read an uplifting scripture, or have a person-to-creator talk with GOD. Another option could be to have a good, gentle, heart cleansing conversation with a very close friend. Something else you might do... volunteer at an agency to help someone young or old who needs your assistance. Being needed can do wonders and leaves very little time for self-pity! Take a walk in the woods, or through a beautiful garden, visit a pet shop or a hospital nursery. Of course you will have to leave me, STRESS, out of these activities as they are not my cup of tea!
(1988)

CLOUDY DAY CHRISTIANS

Why do we wait until we are in way to deep
Then throw our self at the Master's feet?

Why do we wait until we're racked with pain
Before we choose to call the Master's name?

Why do we wait until the day has gone wrong
And then begin singing a Zion song?

Why do we wait until our kids are jailed
The cry "help me Lord", for I have failed?

Why do we stray, our problems never to face
And when things go wrong request amazing grace?

Why are we selfish and un-loving by day
And at night, like saints, we kneel to pray?

Why should we look up with tear-stained eyes
And expect HIM to hear our helpless cries?

Our efforts to serve God must show better labor
Before we expect his mercy and favor

DON'T GIVE UP

Have faith in your inner voice
And life will reveal itself to you
The paths that often seem obscure
Will soon yield meaning to what you do

Stand firm on your convictions
Not allowing your self to stray
Soon the fog of much confusion
Will bow to a brighter day

Cast not away your precious love dreams
Through all disappointments that you see
Someday your heart and mind will know
A love and peace that is meant to be

Turn not away from any stranger
Whom you can give a helping hand
Stretch out your arms and embrace them
Allowing your heart to take a stand

RIDE, RIDE, RIDE

On with that slick second skin
Tights protecting you from the wind
Giving you motive so you can slide
Onto your seat and ride, ride, ride

On with the helmet, on with the gloves
Gives you protection from the shoves
Of the handlebars against your palm
As you whiz through the morning calm

Feels so good with the wind in your face
Feels so good cruising at such a pace
Music pumping from plugged up ears
Taking those hills, shifting those gears

Gives you time to think, time to concentrate
Makes an easy task of working on your weight
Having so much fun, time really flies
Doesn't even feel like doing exercise

Joggers, bikers, skaters out to play
People out walking and getting in your way
Peddling, pumping, easing into the brake
Speeding so smoothly your legs don't ache

Golfers and children playing in the grass
Checking in the mirror before you try to pass
Can't explain the feeling, much too rare

Kind of overdosing on the natural air

Going a little faster, the wind is at your back
Can't stop now, one more turn around the track

Foot just slipped, you take a little tiff
Knowing that tomorrow you'll be a bit stiff
Speaking of tomorrow, got to set some time aside
To recapture this feeling, and just ride, ride, ride.

KEEP TO THE PATH

Freedom of soul and spirit
Is why he died for me
Emancipation means that
I was long ago set free

To use my tools and talents
To achieve all that I can be
To stand up as a role model
For my children to see

My freedom cannot be taken away
He gave me that guarantee
Unless I choose to allow someone
To steal my dignity

I know He is there to assist me
As I call on bended knee
I know I must stay true to self
on the ultimate path to be free

(99-Adrienne)

Ruth Ann Trent

FOR CREW COLUMBIA

Choose your dreams without delay
Now or never, no one can say

Opportunity may knock this one time
Through its window you must climb

Hasten forward do not hesitate
Lest you miss the smile of fate

No future guarantee in any fashion
Just taking bold steps toward your passion

As your talents you boldly pursue…
The Universe graciously welcomes you

02/03

FORGIVENESS

Needs:
A generous heart
to accommodate the act

A promise and an effort never to
repeat the forgiven act

Time...
To deal with our true feelings
To reconcile our hearts
To accept the forgiver
To accept being forgiven

Willingness to...
Be sincere
Be generous
Lack haughtiness
Lack martyrdom
Lack retaliation
Be abundant in humility

It is the act of a mean spirit to hurt others
It is the act of a humble heart to forgive
Forgiveness is not to dismiss or excuse
Forgiveness is to heal the soul

CHOICE

We make excuses... we blame problems on the "world", our environment, our "systems", or anything else we can think of. The bottom line in life is not chance it is **choice.**

When our relationships sour, we blame the other person. The actual fault might be that we allowed them to treat us poorly, or we chose to think so little of ourselves that we did not demand respect, love, or common decency.

Very early on in life we discover how to discern right from wrong. It is one thing to choose to do something wrong and be prepared to take the consequences, but we cannot knowingly make that choice and subsequently place blame on someone or something else.

Choice creates branches on our tree of life. I truly believe there are few junctures without opportunity of choice. Often we gloss over the act or circumstance and quickly utter "I didn't have a choice" but, in retrospect that is not true.

We can *choose* not to teach our children prejudice. We can *choose* to have integrity. We can *choose* to be responsible citizens.

We can *choose* to live the best life we can. We can *choose* to educate ourselves. The choices are endless and we ought to seriously consider and value our <u>freedom</u> of choice.

SPRING FEVER

Today 'tho April raindrops fall
I find I'm not depressed at all
For all my thoughts have turned to Spring
'Cause that's the time I "do my thing"

The clouds are cruising way up high
The flowers smile brightly towards the sky
Men beep their car horns and try to flirt
As I promenade in my mini-skirt

Spring is like a panacea for pain
I suddenly feel alive again
I am so free, I feel youthful too
I want to do things I rarely do

Spring makes me feel like taking a chance
Perhaps to start a new romance
It makes me want busy myself too
Not leaving time for feeling blue

I want to reach for the brightest star above
I want to share an abundance of love
I want to climb to a mountain top and yell
"all of my Winter gloom, go to hell!"

It won't last long it will soon be summer
It will be hot and sticky... a real bummer
Frivolity can't last forever after all
And right around the corner will be fall

I slowly begin not feeling very well
I slowly begin crawling back in my shell
No more energy, zap or zing...
But I will recapture it next Spring!

EPILOGUE

For readers who know me personally, I hope you felt free to add an "amen" here and there. Don't laugh too hard at the Classic 'ISTJ' that is so inherently me.

For readers who know nothing about me, I hope you found some little thing to which you could relate, or something from which you might gain insight.

Who needs therapy when you have writing utensils and paper, or better yet a computer? Although some of the selections included in this publication are from times of struggle, I also write about the abundance and blessings of my life. That is captured in my praise and gratitude journals. Perhaps I will feel comfortable sharing those sometime in the future.

The author

REFERENCES

Pivot Questionnaire – 10 questions originated in a French series, "Bouillon de Culture" hosted by Dr. Bernard Pivot

Mantra – Taken from "In the Spirit" by Susan Taylor
Editor-in-Chief, Essence Magazine

<u>Power of Positive Thinking</u> – Dr. Norman Vincent Peale
Prentice-Hall, Inc. 1952

ISTJ – **I**ntroversion/**S**ensing/**T**hinking/**J**udging - One of 16 personality types identified in the Myers-Briggs Type Indicator (MBTI) Personality Inventory. Isabel Myers and Katherine Briggs developed the assessment based upon the psychological theories of Carl Jung.

ABOUT THE AUTHOR

Ruth Ann was born in New York City and raised in Lambertville, New Jersey. She migrated to the West Coast twenty-three years ago, and now resides in the Puget Sound area in the state of Washington.

Mantra: "I am a child of God, Wise, Guided, Creative, and Loved. I choose Health, Wealth, Happiness, and Sweet Companionship" --

Pivot Questionnaire:

Most favorite word(s)
Panacea and Oxymoron
Least favorite word(s)
I Can't
What turns her on
Music, Music, Music!... and a man with nice thighs
What turns her off
Emotional bullying and intimidation
Sound she loves most
Rain
Sound she hates most
Crying
Favorite curse word
Son-of-a-bitch
Other Profession would like to attempt
Attorney
Other Profession would never like to attempt
Mortician
Wants to hear God Say at the Pearly Gates
You really *CAN* relax, now!

Printed in the United States
63298LVS00001B/58-66